CW00499104

GOLDEN RETRIEVER

Esther Verhoef

GOLDEN RETRIEVER

REBO
PUBLISHERS

© 1999 Rebo International
© 2006 Rebo Publishers

Text and photographs: Esther Verhoef
Cover design and layout: Mesika Design, Hilversum, The Netherlands
Typesetting and pre-press services: A. R. Garamond, Prague,
The Czech Republic
Americanization: David Price for First Edition Translations Ltd,
Cambridge, UK
Proofreading: Sarah Dunham

ISBN 13: 978-90-366-1559-4
ISBN 10: 90-366-1559-3

CONTENTS

1 HISTORY

Of Russian descent?

Golden Retrievers have a balanced and friendly nature

What has been written about the origins of the Golden Retriever demonstrates clearly that the authors, and even those closely involved with the dogs, differ on several issues. In 1914 the English magazine "Country Life" published an article by Arthur Croxton-Smith that described

Golden Retrievers are bred to search for and retrieve animals shot by the hunter

how in 1865 Sir Dudley Marjoribanks, later Lord Tweedmouth, witnessed a performance by a Russian circus in Brighton. Part of the circus program was a group of performing dogs that made such an impression on his Lordship that he bought some of them and decided on a

breeding program which led to today's Golden Retriever. Later, however, one of Lord Tweedmouth's grandsons disputed the Russian origin of these dogs. He claimed that Lord Tweedmouth had indeed been in Brighton, where he had bought a single yellow medium- or long-haired dog from a shoemaker. The dog stood out because of the color of its coat: its brothers and sisters were black. MacLennan, the head gamekeeper on Lord Tweedmouth's estate, Guisachan House in Inverness, was however convinced that Mr. Croxton-Smith's story was true.

Because of these and other contradictory statements it has proven impossible to this day to pinpoint the exact origin of Lord Tweedmouth's Golden Retriever. It is of course quite possible that his Lordship enjoyed fooling his staff and friends, and that he told the less glamorous truth only to his close relatives. We will never be able to discover the real truth, as Lord Tweedmouth died in 1894.

What is certain?

Lord Tweedmouth's kennel records, which he kept from 1835 to 1890, indicate the existence of a yellow dog named Nous. In 1868 Nous covered a bitch named Belle, which is described in the records as a Tweed Water Spaniel. The offspring were four yellow pups, named Crocus, Ada, Primrose, and Cowslip, which were entered in the records as Tweed Water Spaniels. Lord Tweedmouth kept Primrose and Cowslip for himself. Crocus ended up with his son, and Ada was given as a present to the fifth Earl of Chichester. These four dogs are generally recognized as the founders of the pedigree. Golden Retrievers were not bred to type; they did not even carry a uniform name as a breed. Until 1913 they were crossbred with other breeds such as the Bloodhound, other Retrievers, and Setters.

Registration of the pedigree

1913 is an important year in the history of the Golden Retriever. In 1913 an English woman, Mrs. Charlesworth, decided to establish the Golden Retriever Club and a pedigree standard was drawn up. In the same year the British Kennel Club registered the breed pedigree as the Yellow or Golden Retriever. In 1920 this was officially changed to its present name: Golden Retriever.

Right:
The dog probably
owes its fine nose
to the Bloodhound.

2 PEDIGREE STANDARD

The Golden Retriever

General

The hallmark of the Golden Retriever is a kindly and intelligent expression.

The Golden Retriever is well-proportioned. It is active, strong, fluid in its movements, sturdy, and has a kindly expression.

Head

The head of a Golden Retriever is well-proportioned, with beautiful lines blending in well to the neck. The skull is

broad but not heavy. The nose is strong, wide and deep, and usually black. The length of the nasal bone is approximately equal to the length of the skull measured from the clearly distinguishable stop between the eyes to the occipital protuberance. The ears are medium-sized and extend from the level of the eyes. The eyes themselves are dark brown and set well apart, with dark rims. Golden Retrievers have scissor teeth.

Body

Right: a fine example of the breed

The body is symmetrical and well built, with short haunches, a deep chest, curving rib cage, and shoulders long in the blade. The vertebral column forms a straight line. The forelegs are straight and have sturdy bones. The shoulders are sloping. Due to the long shoulder blade and the equally long

arm, the forelegs from the elbow to the ground are well placed below the body. The elbows are positioned close to the body. The haunches and hind legs are very muscular. The knees make a proper angle. The hocks are well let down, and the dog must not be cow-hocked. Seen from behind, the metatarsals make a right angle. The anklebones point neither inward nor outward. Golden Retrievers have feet that are round and cat-like. The tail continues the backbone in a straight line. It reaches to the hocks and does not curl at the tip. The neck is clean and muscular and of a good length.

Height
Dogs have a height at the shoulder of between 22 and 24 inches (56–61 cm), whereas bitches are between 20 and 22 inches (51–56 cm).

Coat and color
The coat of the Golden Retriever can be any shade from golden to cream-colored

The hair is flat or wavy, with good feathering, and the thick undercoat is extremely water-repellent. The coat can be any shade from golden to cream-colored but is neither red nor mahogany. Single white hairs may be found, but only on the chest.

3 THE TYPICAL GOLDEN RETRIEVER

Hounds

Golden retrievers are dogs specialized in finding and retrieving game shot by the hunter, often over water. To carry out this task properly, the dog should love a good swim! A good retriever is not afraid of diving into ice-cold water, even where access to the water is difficult. Furthermore the dog has to be determined to actually find the game; hence considerable stamina is essential. To be successful, the dog has to have an excellent "nose." To avoid damaged game, hunters select their dogs on the criterion of having a "good bite." This means that the dog can take the game in its mouth very carefully without shaking or biting. It also has to get used to gunfire—a dog that becomes nervous or frightened at the noise of a shot may have other outstanding qualities, but as a gun dog it is worthless. Finally, the dog has to be intelligent and should enjoy working for its master.

The Golden Retriever is a dog for people that can offer it an active and varied life.

Right: Golden Retrievers like to retrieve, whether it is game or just a small ball!

Other uses

The Golden Retriever may well be a hunting dog in origin, but the qualities that are so appreciated for the hunt make it also very suitable for other purposes. Golden Retrievers, along with Labradors and German Shepherds, are the dogs most often used as guide dogs for the blind. They are also used to assist people suffering from certain disabilities, being able to deal with such tasks as passing objects to them, switching lights on and off, and opening and shutting doors. Specially trained Golden Retrievers can warn their owners, for instance, when the doorbell rings or when the microwave oven beeps. Due to their hunting instinct and their sense of smell, Golden Retrievers are also often used as rescue dogs. Not every Golden Retriever, however, is suitable for such tasks. Some dogs are more stable and more work-inclined than others. Some organizations breed their new pupils themselves; by using dogs that possess the desired characteristics, the chances are greater that their off-spring can carry out the tasks. Though the Golden Retriever is a quick learner, thorough and prolonged training is necessary before the dog can be deployed.

Family dog

Even though many Golden Retrievers have daily tasks to accomplish, most of them are kept as family dogs. Unfortunately many dog owners seem to forget that their dog loves to do tasks and needs a lot of physical exercise. You will not make a Golden Retriever happy by just taking it for a gentle stroll three times a day, even though it will not protest; it is much too good-natured to do so. Golden Retrievers are really active dogs and suit sports-loving peo-

Idleness will not make the dog a nuisance, but it certainly will not make it any happier.

ple who are fond of going for long walks and have ener-
getic children who would enjoy playing ball games with
the dog. If these conditions are met a Golden Retriever will
definitely be easy to live with.

A social animal
A Golden Retriever is a kind, open-minded and gentle dog
by nature. It socializes with everybody, preferring to be
part of the family and involved in daily routines. Life in a
kennel must feel like a punishment for such a socially
inclined animal!

The Golden Retriever is exceptionally child-friendly. Due
to its great tolerance and poised nature it can put up with a
lot of the things children do. It also has a "good bite"
enabling it to take tidbits offered by children with great
care. Excitement and noise, which always accompany small

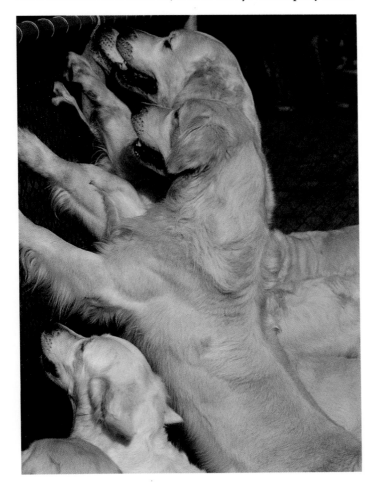

*Mutual problems
about ranking
order are rare
among these dogs.*

children, do not affect its character. Since Golden Retrievers are so good-natured, you will have to teach your children to treat them with respect. Although it is not quick to bite, even for the Golden Retriever enough can be enough. The Golden Retriever is very socially minded. It socializes with everybody, human or animal. Difficulties in ranking order therefore seldom occur among these dogs, neither on the street, nor within the family. If you have acquired your dog from a reputable breeder and you have socialized it properly, you need not anticipate any problems over its attitude to people or other animals.

Guarding

A Golden Retriever seldom barks. If there are trespassers your dog will certainly warn you, but do not expect it to defend you at all costs. Golden Retrievers are not genuine watchdogs or guard-dogs. On the contrary, the vigilance that is a prerequisite for such types of dog is very unwelcome in this breed. On the other hand its loud and sustained barking when it has been startled will drive trespassers away.

Golden Retrievers love water!

Swimming is one of the activities the Golden Retriever most enjoys. It does not care whether it gets soaking wet in a crys-

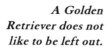

A Golden Retriever does not like to be left out.

tal clear lake on a summer's day or in a muddy pool in rainy and raw weather conditions. A garden pond will quite often be used by the Golden Retriever as a swimming pool. This

liking for water is innate in most Golden Retrievers, and clearly this characteristic does not always help us maintain a spotless home and a clean car. The dog owner should try to understand this, even though a good roll in the mud or a swim on your Golden Retriever's whim should of course not always be allowed. Make sure that your dog listens to your commands, to ensure that you can call it back in time.

A garden pond is irresistible.

Toys

One characteristic of the Golden Retriever is that it loves to carry objects in its mouth. These may consist of a teddy bear, a small ball, or any other item. Your Golden Retriever will carry its favorite object around all day long and will show it proudly to visitors. To prevent your dog walking about with objects you treasure and do not wish to lose, you would do well to buy him a few toys. A puppy might still bite them to pieces, but grown-up dogs will usually treat their toys with care.

Desire to please

The Golden Retriever has an extraordinary desire to please. As a result of the breed's reputation it is often thought that Golden Retrievers need little training, but this usually leads to disappointment. The Golden Retriever is a quick learner anyway—it will quickly master new commands, perform tricks, and do whatever else you would like to teach it. But... it remains a dog with its own proper personality, which can be stubborn and even awkward on occasion. A pheasant flying up, an inviting muddy ditch, the smell of a bitch in heat, adolescence—all of these are situations in which even a Golden Retriever may forget its training and follow its instincts instead.

Disobedience may be caused by a physical defect, or may result from boring or inadequate training. Do not expect your puppy to be a "super-dog" that understands everything it is asked to do and obeys like a machine. A pedigree Golden Retriever has all the qualities you could wish for, but how many of these qualities it will actually display depends on you.

A typical situation: a Golden Retriever carrying an object in its mouth

4 THE PURCHASE

Things to bear in mind

The many advantages of having a dog have probably already crossed your mind. There are also disadvantages. Keeping a dog of whatever breed as a pet entails lots of work. If you should want to go away for a weekend or longer, then someone has to look after the dog. In some cases the dog may be able to accompany you, but often you

A dog of any breed entails lots of work.

Right: Who could resist this?

will need someone to look after the animal, or boarding kennels.

The dog itself will of course also need care. A Golden Retriever's coat has to be brushed and combed every other day, and in addition a visit should be paid to the grooming parlor once or twice a year for a trim. Every dog can suffer from fleas, and effective flea-killers are often expensive. Furthermore, the dog should be vaccinated annually and treated for worms twice a year. A dog may of course fall ill, and in some cases lengthy and expensive veterinary care may be necessary. Hence the purchase price of a dog will be only a fraction of what the dog will cost you during its lifetime. The point to remember is that from the first day the puppy arrives at your home it will strongly influence your daily routines for at least 12 years. It is a living being which is entirely dependent on you for its well-being. So think very carefully whether you want to, and are able to, provide this new member of your family with a good life.

A dog or a bitch

There are some important differences between owning a dog and owning a bitch. Bitches are in season twice a year for a period of three weeks, during which time they attract

The choice between a dog (on the right) and a bitch is very personal.

dogs and can be made pregnant. If you own a bitch but do not like the idea of her being in heat at certain times of the year you might consider having her spayed. Periodic injections can be a temporary remedy in coping with a bitch in heat. Bear in mind that bitches only think about procreation twice a year, whereas dogs are available all year round. Golden Retrievers possess an excellent sense of smell and sexually mature dogs can smell a bitch in heat from a great distance. It may cause them to behave in an unusual way for several days. Bitches usually only urinate when they need to and they do it squatting. Dogs usually urinate against objects and will also plant scent markings, normally in your own garden. Dogs have a more stable character than bitches since they are not influenced by shifts in their hormonal balance. Finally there is also the difference in size: bitches are generally smaller and less heavily built than dogs.

A puppy or a more mature dog?
Most people will choose a puppy rather than a mature animal. They feel they can train a puppy to be the dog they want. There is no flaw in that argument—except that puppies inherit a personality of their own which their owner can influence but probably not change.

Three generations

A puppy is not a blank piece of paper on which you can write whatever you please. For people that dislike the idea of having to raise and house-train a puppy, an older dog that has been given a good education elsewhere could be the right choice. Older dogs usually adapt to new circumstances really well and will become attached to you and your family just as a puppy would. These dogs are usually already house-trained, have left their adolescence behind them, and will be acquainted with several commands. If you choose to have an older dog you should inquire about the dog's history. Think carefully if you suspect the dog has any mental or physical defects. Dogs that have spent most of their life in kennels can usually learn to adapt to life in a family home, but they will need to have an owner with a lot of patience and understanding.

A puppy is fun, but you can get just as much enjoyment from an older dog

Various bloodlines

Character traits are partly hereditary, and this is also true for looks and capacities for certain disciplines. The chances of coming across a good gun dog among a litter of pups of which the parents and grandparents have previously performed well as gun dogs will of course be higher than if

If your ambition is to enter shows, you would do best to pick your dog from a so-called "show strain"

you try your luck selecting a puppy from a litter where the parents and ancestors have been predominantly chosen for their looks. Such factors are important if you have plans to start breeding, to enter shows, or to enroll your future companion in gun-dog training sessions. One does not exclude the other, however—there are plenty of serious breeders who pay attention to both looks and the capacity for work. Even so, if you have particular plans for the future, it would be wise to inquire extensively through a breeders' association beforehand.

Popular dogs

Golden Retrievers are tremendously popular. The demand for puppies is so great that you may have to wait six months or more to acquire one from a good breeder. Not everybody is that patient, which is why some people decide to try a different breed. Be very wary about purchasing a puppy from handlers who are unknown to the breeders' association.

Various partly hereditary defects of the breed are apparent, such as elbow problems, hip dysplasia, and eye abnormalities. Good breeders are aware of these defects and submit their breeding animals for testing in order to detect them. If a dog's health is not of the best, it should be excluded from further breeding. As a result of the breed's popularity there are unfortunately quite a few breeders interested only in making money. Whether the pups they have bred are healthy and whether their character and looks are typical of the breed are matters of little concern to them. You may of course be lucky enough to find a reliable breeder, but there is a strong chance that you will go home with a pup that once grown up or maybe even earlier will fail to meet your expectations, and which might have inherited a problem.

The Golden Retriever is a very popular breed.

To ensure that the pup you purchase has every chance genetically of growing into a healthy dog with a character typical of the breed, you would be wise to contact the puppy section of the Golden Retriever Club of America. This association can put you in touch with puppy referral volunteers who will advise on reliable breeders. You will find the contact details at the back of this book.

What should you watch out for?

If you decide to purchase a dog without consulting the breed club, you will have to be aware of potential problems. Always ask for the pedigree and other papers so that you can see whether or not both parent dogs have been checked for diseases that occur among Golden Retrievers. Make sure that you are familiar with these papers and what the test results actually mean. You may ask a veterinarian for advice, or you can of course ask for advice from the breed club. Do not be impressed by such terminology as "descended from a champion," as this phrase may be used even when there is no champion whatsoever to be found in the pedigree. Be also very wary if the breeder goes overboard in praising the pup's qualities. It is very natural that a breeder should be proud of his or her pups, but a serious breeder will be far more interested in whether or not you can offer the pup a good home than in the fee. When you see the breeding box, pay particular attention to how the breeder treats the animals. This may tell you its own story. Also closely watch the behavior of the mother dog. As it feels responsible for its pups it may react in rather a restrained way. However, if it reacts suspiciously, or is frightened or behaves

The mother dog should make a stable and friendly impression.

nervously, then this is a sure sign of difficulties ahead. Such behavioral problems may or may not be hereditary, but an unstable bitch is still not a good example for its offspring. Last but not least pay attention to the pups' own behavior. If they are not sleepy, they will be eager to make your acquaintance. Healthy pups are outgoing, they like to play and are curious about their surroundings. Pups that withdraw, that are shy, or even bashful or apathetic, are better not taken home. Pay attention also to how the pups look. A protruding belly may be caused by a worm infection but may also be the result of the pups just having had a good meal. A mangy coat, with evidence of fleas, covered in dirt, weeping eyes and nose, and traces of diarrhea are never good signs. Finally, a Golden Retriever pup should feel firm and look compact.

Imprinting

From birth to adulthood a puppy goes through several stages. One of the most important stages is the phase of imprinting. During this phase, which extends from about the third to the seventh week of its life, a puppy for the first time becomes aware of the world around it. It becomes acquainted with the everyday things of life, especially noises and smells. It is

A puppy should grow up in an environment that allows it to encounter the outside world.

picked up and cuddled, and it learns that people will not harm it. It hears the sound of the radio, the noise of the vacuum cleaner, the sounds of children playing, and it learns not to be afraid of them. A pup that has not gone through these experiences during this phase will grow up to be an angst-ridden, apathetic dog that will never function as a family dog. These extreme behavioral disturbances are there to stay. An effective period of imprinting is therefore of the utmost importance. A puppy that stays indoors during the early days of its life does not need imprinting. It will get used to the world around it in a natural way. Pups that grow up in a kennel or some other secluded area must be put in touch with the everyday things of life for at least 15 minutes a day. A good breeder knows this and takes his or her responsibility for it seriously.

The choice

If you go to see a litter that has not yet been vaccinated, it is probable the breeder will not want you to pick up the pups, to touch or even come close to them. This might seem very unfriendly, but it says much in favor of the breeder: in fact he is being careful with the puppies' health. The breeder cannot know where you have been earlier that day. You may carry dis-

If you find it difficult to make a choice, ask your breeder for his or her opinion.

It quickly gets its coat dry after a swim.

eases with you of which you are unaware and thus contaminate the pup. Pups that have been vaccinated do not have to be handled so carefully. It is not true that you should always choose the first pup that comes up to you. Even though dogs themselves also have their own preferences, well-reared and healthy pups will all move toward you. The first one to bite your shoelaces will also be the most dominant and daring of the litter, hence during its training it will usually demand more understanding and authority from you. In most litters there will also be a puppy that will approach you with greater caution and apparent shyness. Such a puppy will usually not function very well among a lively family, but it will thrive in a more peaceful environment with a quiet owner. If you find it difficult to make up your mind, follow the breeder's advice. He (or she) has handled the puppies on a day-to-day basis and should be able to point out the puppy that will suit you best, based on your expectations and a description of your family situation.

Papers

A pup is best moved to its new owner when it is eight to nine weeks old. If the puppy has not yet been tattooed or micro-chipped at that time, you will have to be a little more patient. Micro-chipping and tattooing is usually carried out between the sixth and ninth weeks. The breeder may not yet be able to provide you with a pedigree, as it needs some time for the administration to be completed. Many breeders will send you the pedigree later, possibly some months later. If by chance you purchase your pup from an address unknown to the breed society or the Kennel Club, make absolutely sure that your dog has been tattooed or micro-chipped when you take it home. Without a tattoo or a chip your pup will not be eligible for a pedigree.

Early days
Ask the breeder if you may have a piece of cloth that has been in the whelping box. You can put this piece of cloth in the new indoor kennel or basket, where the familiar smell will reassure the puppy. You should always receive a vaccination certificate indicating the kind of vaccinations provided, when they were carried out, and when they have to be repeated. The breeder will provide you with a health certificate. This certificate is a declaration by a veterinarian that the pup was healthy at the time of the checkup and that no physical defects were apparent. Every good breeder will also supply you with a diet sheet and in many cases a small container of the food the pup is used to eating as well. The diet sheet will give you guidelines about the kind of food that you can provide for your dog, and it should indicate quantities and feeding times. It is advisable to follow these guidelines during the first few months. Probably you will also be given a contract of purchase stating the rights and obligations of both the seller and the purchaser. Check that the terms of the contract are reasonable before you sign anything.

A puppy about four months old

5 YOUR PUPPY AT HOME

A new home

When you have collected your pup from the breeder, it is best to give it the opportunity to urinate before you take it into your home. Find a special corner in your own garden for this. Since your puppy has probably not had all its vaccinations, it may become infected and catch a disease if it comes into contact with the germs that are likely to be found in the urine and excrement of other dogs. This is why you should avoid places where other dogs go before the age of 12 weeks, by which time your pup should have

Far right: you should always use two hands to hold your puppy.

received all its vaccinations. When your pup enters your home for the first time you should let it sniff around for a while. Do not call it, do not run after it, and tell your children to disturb it as little as possible.

Remember that everything is new to the puppy. It has to absorb so many new sensations that too much attention

The first night can be an ordeal; many pups will start to howl.

would tire it out. Make sure that some water is available and that the dog can find it. Show it its sleeping place with the cloth from the breeder in it, and help it to recognize this place as its bed. Pups need a lot of sleep and should not be disturbed while sleeping. If you have children they have to learn to leave their new friend in peace while it sleeps or when it retreats to its indoor kennel or basket. Teach them also not to pick it up and drag it around. Tranquility and a regular life are of the utmost importance for your puppy during the first weeks.

The first night

The first, but often also the second and third night, can be a real ordeal—for the pup as well as for you. Many pups howl desperately when they realize they have been left alone. This is a very natural reaction. You should however not allow your puppy's call for help—which is what it actually is—to be successful. Otherwise your pup will think that it can always end its solitude by making a lot of noise. The chances then are that it will continue this behavior, even when it has grown up, every time it does not want to be alone. It does not care whether you comfort it, shout at it in anger from your bed, or punish it. It wanted company and it succeeded. By holding back during the first few nights you will prevent your dog developing difficult behavior that cannot be cured afterward. Sometimes a warm hot-water bottle wrapped in a cloth that smells of the whelping box may solve the problem. Surrounded by warmth and the smell of its old bed your puppy will fall asleep more quickly.

A crate

One of the most convenient things that you can buy for your puppy is a spacious crate. A crate used to be popular

mostly among breeders, but nowadays the general dog owner has come to perceive its value.
Crates exist in various sizes and materials: from crates almost completely made out of wire to plastic crates with a little door at the front. They are strong enough to prevent

An indoor kennel or crate is extremely useful when it comes to education and house-training.

your puppy—or mature dog—biting through and escaping. Crates are not cheap and therefore many owners are reluctant to purchase one.

Remember though that your lovely carpet or the couch into which your pup might sink its teeth will be much more expensive. Moreover, the pup will make its owner very angry by such actions, which do not contribute to mutual understanding. An extra advantage is that your pup will not have a chance to bite through electric wires or nibble at poisonous plants while it is in its crate. If the crate is spacious enough for an adult Golden Retriever to lie down comfortably in, you will enjoy its use for many years. You can also use the crate to take your dog in your car, and this is certainly much safer than transporting it loose on the back seat of the car. Anyway, a crate is not a dog cage. The idea behind it is that you can temporarily put your dog away in a safe place at those moments when you have no time to keep an eye on it. The crate is also a perfect aid for house-training, as mentally healthy pups do not dirty their sleeping place.

Right: Shining with self-confidence and with a well-groomed gleaming coat

Never use a crate as a disciplinary tool, but introduce it in a positive manner. Line it with a comfortable, washable cloth and put a safe and interesting toy or chewing bone inside that the pup only uses in its crate. In this way you make its stay in the crate a lot more attractive. You will eventually notice your dog going to its crate by itself when it wants to sleep or lie down.

6 HOUSE-TRAINING

Smells

Pups are house-trained by nature. While they are with the breeder, if they are kept in a spacious and tidy place they will usually not dirty the nest. This would be against their instincts. What you should teach your pup at this moment is to regard your house and other people's houses as its nest. To house-train it successfully it is best during the first weeks to always walk the pup in the same area. Dogs have

Puppies recognize their own scent out of thousands.

Right: if you pay attention to it a Golden Retriever will usually be house-trained quickly

an excellent sense of smell and are also creatures of habit. The scent of urine or excrement produced earlier will encourage them to repeat it in the same place; they will even prefer to do so. This is also true indoors. Its excellent nose will enable your Golden Retriever to recognize its own smell through all kinds of detergents and air fresheners.

Signs

You may assume that pups will move their bowels after they have eaten and just after they have woken up. Before it will urinate or defecate, your pup will often sniff and turn round. It is looking for the right place. When you notice your pup behaving like this you should immediately pick it up and take it outside. There is usually no point in calling your pup outside since the urge might be too much for it on its way out. At first it is certainly not a bad thing to take your puppy outside every hour.

At night

It is best to leave your pup in its crate during the night. As by nature your puppy will not dirty this place, it is a good idea to make the nights shorter during the first weeks. Walk your dog at night as late as possible so as to let it start the night with an empty stomach, and get up a few hours earlier in the morning. The first weeks you can set your alarm in order to put it outside for a while halfway through the night. You must of course remove its feeding and drinking bowls.

Punishment and rewards

Your Golden Retriever really wants to please you, but it has to know how to do so. It will learn this from the rewards that you give it when it does something properly. So never forget to greet your dog encouragingly in a cheerful high-pitched voice whenever it empties its bowels outdoors. It used to be common practice to punish dogs that made a mistake inside the house, but we know nowadays that this actually led to a lot of problems in the field of house-training. If you catch a dog on the spot and then punish it immediately afterward, it might get the impression that you do not want it to empty its bowels in front of you. This will cause your pup to try very hard to empty its bowels without you noticing it. Kept on the leash it will not make any effort, but once it is indoors it will start looking for a quiet corner. Therefore it is better not to take any notice of accidents. If you catch your dog misbehaving, just pick it up and take it outside. If it continues to relieve itself, then reward it. Punishing it afterward should be avoided. Dogs link punishment and reward to the exact moment when they are punished or rewarded. Punishing it for urinating or defecating some time earlier will make your dog think you are shouting at it for no reason at all. With a sensitive pup such punishment will produce fear of the inconsistent master and disturb the mutual bond between the two. In general you can get your puppy house-trained quickly without a problem and without punishing it. Reward it whenever it behaves well and try to prevent it from making mistakes indoors as much as possible by watching carefully and by using a crate at times.

Many young dogs will urinate out of sheer joy at their master's return home.

Excitement urination

Young dogs do not yet have full control over their bladder, for which you cannot always blame them. There are a few ways of not being house-trained that actually have nothing to do with house-training at all. One of these is urinating out of pleasure that you have come home. The joy at your arrival is overwhelming, hence making the dog lose control over its bladder. It is pointless to punish your puppy for this. It hardly notices itself urinating and it cannot help itself either. Most dogs will outgrow this phase. If you find it very awkward, when you get home, call your dog outside where it cannot do any harm. The greater the emotion, the earlier a dog will urinate. Hence it is sensible not to make a big thing of your arrival and to cuddle it really well outside a little later.

Submissive urination

Another form of not being house-trained is submissive urination. This is the most extreme gesture of submission a dog has at its disposal. We notice this form of urination often in dogs that are already rather submissive by nature, often in combination with an over-dominant master. With some dogs, just one look from their master will be enough to make them roll over on their backs and urinate. With other pups this behavior will particularly occur when they are punished. If your dog often urinates submissively, think about your own behavior toward it. A gentler attitude will lead to improvement with dogs that regard your leadership as intimidating.

Emptying its bowels on command

The Golden Retriever has a superb nose.

At a time when a dog's mess on the sidewalk is a source of irritation for many, and this irritation is leading to a harsher and more stringent municipal policy on dogs, teaching your puppy to empty its bowels only in places where it is allowed to do so is not only an obligation to your neighbors but also something you owe to other dog-owners. This is by no means very difficult for you or a nuisance to your dog—far from it. First, go to a dog-walking area or a dog toilet,

where the dog can empty its bowels. Then take it out for a good walk without the worry that something might happen. Obviously it is important not to leave home late. Do not treat the "command" as seriously as commands such as "Sit" and "Stay." If your dog feels no need, it cannot "produce," not even on command.

Since young dogs do not yet have full control over their bladders, small mistakes may happen during the first five or six months. The small word that you link to defecating on command is thus a friendly request. You will teach your dog this request by using it every time your pup excretes. You could for instance say "busy," which should be followed always by a friendly and approving: "that's a good dog." To begin with you use the word when your pup has defecated on its own initiative. Later on you take it with you to the dog-walking place where you say the word as soon as it starts to sniff around. Reward it with "that's a good dog" when it has indeed emptied its bowels. After a while your dog will link the request to the action, thus only saying the word in the dog-walking area will be enough.

A young dog can learn to defecate on command.

When a house-trained dog suddenly starts to behave as if it were not house-trained, there is usually a medical reason such as diabetes, a bladder infection, or a kidney disorder causing it.

7 ORDER OF RANKING AND BODY LANGUAGE

Behavior of the pack

In the wild, dogs live in packs and thus they prefer to be part of a group. A dog therefore only feels comfortable and is happy when there is a clear order of precedence in the group. The pack leader will ensure that its subordinates have everything they need, but demands some privileges in return which the lower ranking will not have. A pack leader may for instance correct its subordinates, it may stay, sit, and lie down wherever and whenever it wants to, it eats

Right: your Golden Retriever will look upon your family as its pack.

before the others, and will indicate when, for how long, and where a walk will lead to. Such rules are not man-made. With dogs this behavior is partly inherited, partly acquired. Pups learn the most important rules of the "pecking order" from their mother and by playing with the other pups in their litter. Your new house guest will naturally regard your family as its pack. The roles in the pack are not divided naturally and will have to be enforced intentionally by you. In some families the dog has become the leader of the pack; it pulls on its leash and corrects its "subordinates" by growling and even snarling when it does not like their conduct. Grooming the coat of such a dog is an enormous task as it is forced into a submissive position that does not go with its rank order. In such unusual circumstances the dog will often be thought to be in the wrong, while this is evidently not the case. The fact is, a dog can only follow its instincts. If it does not see its lenient and inconsistent master as the pack leader, it will decide to take over for the benefit of the pack, with all the consequences.

The leader of the pack

Luckily, a Golden Retriever is not very dominant by nature. The chances of a Golden Retriever taking over the role of pack leader from you are not very high given the generally friendly nature of this dog. However, in the interest of your dog and your family it is important to set clear boundaries. For a great deal of its self-confidence it relies on the peace, order, and transparency that prevail in the group, and it will without doubt start to feel insecure if you treat it inconsistently and are unclear. Many behavioral problems may then occur, such as destructive, anxious, or servile behavior, dirtiness, and disobedience. Therefore it is very important that you should take a stand as a consistent and indisputable leader of the pack. Let your dog know every day that it ranks the lowest in your family. If you and the rest of the family consistently apply the following rules, they will bring about the peace and transparency that the dog demands from you.

- Do not allow the dog free access to the entire house. This privilege is reserved for the other family members, as they rank higher than the dog. Upstairs serves perfectly as forbidden territory for your dog, especially as going upstairs is not good for its system.
- Only feed the dog when everybody else has finished eating. The higher ranks always eat first. You can also feed your dog at times not immediately before or after your own mealtimes.
- When you arrive home, greet your family members first and the dog last. The higher ranking is greeted first, the lower ranking last. The condition for a cuddle or a gentle stroke is however that your dog comes to greet you of its own accord.
- Always walk in front; your dog will follow. Never let your dog decide where the walk will lead to, and never let it walk in front of you through a door or entering a room. The pack leader walks in front, the lower rank follows.
- Do not stroke your dog or play with it when it tries to force you into it. It is commanding you to take notice of it, thus indulging in the role of the leader.
- Never lie on the floor, but always keep your face in a higher position than the head of the dog. A higher rank literally never takes a lower position than a subordinate. Always call your dog to you and never walk toward it.
- A higher rank never walks toward someone ranking lower, it should always be the other way around.

Children and the order of ranking

Golden Retrievers are well known for their high tolerance when it concerns children. Nevertheless sometimes things may go wrong, usually because the dog receives the wrong signals or because it is bothered or teased. In order to avoid the relationship between your children and your dog deteriorating, you will have to teach your children:

- ⊨ Always to call the dog toward them and never to approach it themselves (or even worse to crawl toward it);
- ⊨ Never to tease the dog;
- ⊨ Not to yell, argue, or run away when the dog is near;
- ⊨ To leave the dog in peace when it is eating or sleeping;
- ⊨ Not to command it unnecessarily or inconsistently;
- ⊨ Not to lie on the floor, and always to keep their face in a higher position than the dog's head;
- ⊨ Not to stare at the dog.

Children and dogs can teach each other many things and often become friends for life.

It is impossible to teach these rules to very young children. Therefore for safety's sake never leave them alone with the dog. The precise age at which your child will be old enough to be left alone with the dog or to walk it, cannot be set. It just depends on the dog's strength and character as well as the physical strength, superiority, and sense of responsibility of your child.

Dog language

In order to know what is in your dog's mind, you will have to learn to understand the intentions behind its behavior. This book cannot include a discussion of all the aspects of dog language, but several excellent books have been written on this subject that are certainly worth reading. We will limit ourselves at this point to behavior used by dogs to tell us and to tell each other whether they are dominant or subordinate in certain situations. The body language of dogs can be observed clearly when your dog meets another dog or human being. Characteristic for a dominant posture are a tail carried aloft and ears that are erect. The dog will try to make itself appear larger and will keep its head and neck as high as possible. It may lay its head on top of the other dog's neck, back, or head in order to emphasize its status. A dog which in this particular situation regards itself as being of lower rank will take on a subordinate posture. It will lower its head, the ears will be folded back, and the tail is kept below the back line or even stuck between the legs. In a highly threatening situation a submissive dog will roll

Submissive attitude: ears folded back and posture close to the ground

Two dogs meeting

over on its back and may spill some urine, the most extreme form of submission. It may very well be that a dog shows submissive behavior toward members of the family while it takes up a dominant posture when interacting with other dogs. Its attitude may also differ from dog to dog and from person to person, as for each particular situation.

The function of urine and feces

In interaction between dogs urine and feces play an important role. Not only the smell but also the place where urine or feces is found will convey a message from the sender. In particular the conduct of dogs that are very self-confident stands out. Thus dominant dogs will put out their scent markings as high as possible. Male dogs will raise one of their hind legs for this and highly dominant bitches may occasionally raise a hind leg, even though this is rare.

Usually a hole is scratched fiercely in the ground afterward. In this way the scent is spread and the higher status is confirmed. Furthermore, the place where the feces are dropped may indicate the status of the sender. It is not uncommon for dominant dogs to look for a molehill or other higher positioned place to deposit their feces.

Scents play an important role in the communication between dogs.

8 EDUCATION

The process of socializing

The phase of socializing follows the imprinting phase and will continue until the age of about 14 weeks. Hence your dog will go through this stage when it has already become part of your family. During this phase your dog is very open to new impressions, which will determine its attitude toward the surrounding world for the rest of its life. To everything that it becomes familiar with during this period it will react in a balanced way later on in its life. Therefore it is particularly important that your pup comes across as many different people, animals, and objects as possible. Do not overstate the importance of new situations, hence introduce them quietly as something very natural. When you take your dog for example to a busy street, do not stop if it reacts anxiously. Just keep on walking and

If the socialization phase is properly managed, your dog will become a well-balanced animal.

Right: A consistent approach will bring you an obedient and happy dog.

briefly pull the leash short to show your dog what your intentions are.

Make sure that your dog understands that you are self-confident, regardless of the situation. React in exactly the same way as you would do without your dog. Your dog will then

You are the best example for your dog.

copy your relaxed and self-assured attitude. Do not however expose your dog to too many impressions as this may work against it. Another bridge can be crossed the day after.

Negative experiences during the socialization phase
If conditions are favorable, your puppy will acquire only positive experiences during its socialization phase. You cannot always however avoid a negative incident happening. Such incidents may be remembered by your dog for its entire life, especially if they occur during this susceptible period. Be aware that you, the pack leader, are the best example and that your reaction and attitude toward the event will be decisive for your dog. If by chance something negative happens, just react calmly and with understatement whenever possible. Do not stand still, do not shout, do not pick your puppy up, and do not comfort it! When its leader acts indecisively or panics, your puppy will have a really good reason to get anxious. The incident will be fixed in its memory, and this may eventually lead to a neurotic dog. It is not really the incident itself but in particular how the master reacts to it that determines how your pup will react to such events for the rest of its life.

Foresight is the essence of government
Your Golden Retriever will be part of your life for at least ten years and probably longer. You cannot know what your situation will be in ten years' time. Perhaps you may live in a house with a garden at present, but in a few years' time it might be

an apartment with an elevator. If your dog is not used to elevators it could have problems adapting to one. Maybe you will have children, cats, or other animals in a couple of years, or you will be using public transportation more often, etc. This is why you should use the socialization period fully and also get your pup acquainted with things that are less obvious. You and your dog can derive much benefit from this in the future.

Being consistent
Only by being consistent at all times can you rear an obedient and happy dog. You may do everything according to the book, but if the rules you apply are flexible it will all be quite useless. Before your puppy enters your home you will have to agree with the members of your family what the dog may and may not do. Think this over carefully. If you think it is all right for your dog to lie on the couch, you should also allow this when it is soaking wet from the rain. If you have decided that your dog may not leap up at people, then likewise do not allow this when it is still small or when you are wearing old clothes. If you do not want to have a begging dog, only give it food in its feeding bowl and do not feed it from your table or from the kitchen worktop. The small differences that make us decide to sometimes allow behavior and other times not, are just impossible for your dog to comprehend. An inconsistent approach is very confusing—your dog will not be able to distinguish between what is allowed and what is not allowed. It is only logical that it will try to leap up at you or to lie on the couch over and over again, and that it will keep on staring at the plate of peanuts for hours and hours, saliva dripping from its mouth. In all too many cases, irritating behavior and disobedience are the result of the master being inconsistent—or to put it another way: you are not in control. Being consistent is certainly not easy, but your endeavors will be rewarded by a cheerful, obedient dog that knows its limits and will not go beyond them.

Punishment and rewards
During the dog's education you will use punishment and rewards. It is essential that the dog should know when it is actually being punished or rewarded. This seems to be childishly obvious, but in practice many dog-owners appear to find it difficult. The words "that's a good dog" are mumbled, or the dog receives a casual stroke on the top of the head—and that is all. To punish seems equally difficult. "Naughty dog" is said a couple of times and the leash is pulled casually, but the dog hardly reacts and continues its unacceptable behavior. In both cases the message the owner wants to convey to the dog is not properly understood by the animal. Therefore reward and punish very clearly. Pronounce loudly and clear-

ly either your praise ("that's a good dog") or your angry words ("naughty dog") as if there were an exclamation point after them. The pitch of your voice is also extremely important. Use a high-pitched cheerful voice when you reward it and a low-pitched gruff voice when you punish it. Make a

The Golden Retriever is a very sensitive dog. A harsh approach is out of the question.

fuss of it when you express your praise, fondle and cuddle it with enthusiasm, and give it the idea that it has just performed tremendously well. You will see from the way your dog reacts if you have got through to it or not.

Good timing

Your Golden Retriever should understand not merely that it is being punished or rewarded, but also for what reason. In practice, good timing seems not to be easy for many owners. Your dog links punishment and reward to what it is doing at the present moment. Suppose your dog has turned your living room into a mess while you were away. You arrive home, your dog walks toward you in a happy mood, and then you start bellowing at it. The dog does not see the connection between you bursting with anger and the mess that it has caused, but it will think that your outburst has something to do with your arrival and the fact that it walked cheerfully toward you. So what will happen next time you come home? Your dog will wait expectantly in a somewhat depressed state, its ears folded back. It will submissively walk toward you or it will stay where it is. Maybe by chance it has broken something again. This time you will not see a dog with a submissive attitude, but one that you think is perfectly aware of its guilt. If this example seems familiar to you then there is only one proper solution, which is to make sure that your dog simply does not have a chance to do anything naughty while you are out. Thus it will always be "good dog" when

Left in a crate or indoor kennel while you are out, your dog will not have the opportunity to get dirty or to break things.

you arrive home. The best thing to do is to put it in an indoor kennel. Destructive behavior is often an expression of boredom. More physical exercise and things to do sometimes improve the situation. Good timing is also important when training. If for example you give the command "Sit," your dog will start to sit down. Do not praise it yet, as you would then be rewarding it for its intention. Only when it really sits down is it a "good dog" —not earlier than that!

Choke leash

Choke chains and choke leashes

In general, Golden Retrievers can easily be controlled by your voice. Nevertheless situations can occur in which your voice alone will not be enough. In such cases a choke leash can be very useful to emphasize your words. By pulling briefly but firmly on the choke leash you will imitate a disciplinary bite on the neck. This is a bite that a higher-ranking dog will give to a subordinate when the latter makes a mistake. Make sure that the end of the leash goes over the top of the neck, and not underneath. A properly adjusted leash will open again immediately after being pulled and will not bother the dog.

Displacement behavior

Displacement behavior is often displayed by dogs that experience too much pressure during training. Through such behavior they seek to delay obeying the command received. Instead of responding directly to your command, it urinates, yawns, or rolls over on its back. Whenever your dog behaves like this, just play with it for a while and conclude the exercise with a command that it is familiar with and responds well to. Then end the training.

When a dog rolls on its back this may be form of displacement behavior.

9   BASIC TRAINING

Getting used to a collar

The most suitable collar for your Golden Retriever is made of soft but indestructible nylon. Do not buy a collar that allows for growth, but make sure that it fits properly so as to prevent your puppy from chewing the end of it or wrenching itself free while you are out on the street. Putting the collar on for the first time just before you feed it or just before you start playing with it, will make the puppy accept it faster. As soon as it is accustomed to wearing the collar you can attach a light leash. Let your puppy walk around for a while like this under supervision, until it is used to this as well. Next you can hold the end of the leash and with an encouraging voice and a tidbit you persuade the dog to go with you.

Golden Retrievers quickly get used to wearing a collar and leash.

A successful education

Right: Make sure that your dog understands what you mean.

You as a person can ensure that your pup grows up as an obedient and happy animal by observing some very important guidelines.

Young pups are easily distracted. Do not overwork them during training.

Be consistent
Consistency should be at the heart of everything, especially during training. So do not change an earlier command and never be satisfied with a command only half carried out. Always conclude a training session with a command that has been properly obeyed.

You are the one to change a command — not your dog
If you have given the command "Down" and the puppy leaves its position after just a couple of seconds, it has changed the command. This is not your puppy's prerogative. It is you that changes the command by saying "Get up" or "Go."

Do not overwork
Your puppy is frisky and easily distracted. You cannot yet expect it to lie or sit down for five minutes without moving. Change the command after a couple of seconds and steadily extend the time it lasts. In that way it will not be tempted to be disobedient.

Keep your pup motivated
A pup that enjoys the training learns faster and remembers better. Therefore never train for long periods at a time. To begin with, five or ten minutes will be long enough. Alternate the commands with periods of play and never forget to reward it when it has per-

formed well. Nothing will motivate a pup more than a master clearly pleased with its behavior.

Be clear
Pronounce your commands clearly and start by stating the pup's name to ensure that it knows that you are talking to it.

Choose the right moment
Do not train when your pup has not yet eaten, when its bladder is full, or when it is drowsy. Only give it a command when its attention is focused on you. If it is distracted, your command will scarcely make any impression on it. This is why you should train in a quiet place with as little distraction as possible.

Do not repeat unnecessarily
"Goldie, down. Sit down, go and sit down. Goldie no..., down, I really mean it, you know." If you command your dog in such a way, your words will lose their meaning. First get its attention by calling its name, only then give the command once, loud and clear.

The command "Come!"
The first and maybe also the most important command that you can teach a young pup is the command "Come!" On your cheerfully spoken command your pup should quickly walk toward you. Attach a long lightweight leash to the collar and

Make sure that you gain the puppy's full attention before giving a command.

let your dog play and sniff around without you pulling on the leash. Call it by its name, followed by the command "Come!" Make it particularly interesting for the pup to come toward you by squatting while you invitingly tap your hands on the ground. If your pup immediately walks toward you it is only natural that you will praise it generously and maybe give it a reward. If it does not come immediately, even though you are certain that it has heard your command, just repeat the command more loudly followed by a brief but not a hard pull on the leash. Basically, a Golden Retriever puppy will learn this command very quickly. Once your pup knows this command properly you can continue practicing on a safe and enclosed terrain without a leash.

Mistakes while coming to you
At a later stage, from the time your puppy becomes an adolescent, the command "Come!" may cause difficulties. Instead of chasing after your dog—a game you are bound to

Why come? I haven't finished playing yet.

lose, as your dog becomes faster at running and turning—you would do better, when the puppy takes no notice of your command, to squat and ignore it or walk away in the opposite direction. Most dogs will then come to you all too quickly. Remember, even if your Golden Retriever only obeys your command after several tricks and long delays, it is still a "good dog." After all, it obeyed in the end, even if it took a while. Preferably, do not call it when it is busy doing something it enjoys, for it will learn that "Come!" is equal to "stop the fun," whereas it should actually want to enjoy being with its master. If you cannot avoid putting an end to its fun, let it go after it has come to you or play with it for a while before you go home.

The command "Bed"
You can also teach your pup the command "Bed" at an early age. After you have given it this command, it has to look quickly for its sleeping-place (the basket or crate) and stay there. It goes without saying that this command can best be taught to the pup when it is already fairly tired. It will then be a lot more motivated. Put your pup in its crate or basket and give it the command "Bed." If your dog stays in its crate or basket, whether it be standing or lying, you should reward it immediately. If it immediately leaves its place, you say "No! Bed!" and put it back in its place. As soon as it understands what you mean by your command it will often just be enough to utter the command and to point at its basket or crate.

The command "Sit" can easily be taught with the help of a small treat.

The command "Sit"
Learning to sit on command can usually be taught quickly and easily to a Golden Retriever. Hold a small tidbit just above its nose and give it the command "Sit." You will notice that in its enthusiasm to get the tidbit it will often sit down spontaneously. If it does not do this then make your intentions clear by lightly pushing down its haunches. Give it the piece of cheese immediately when it sits and praise it. If your pup can already sit on command you can teach it to sit at every curb, even when there are no cars passing. It will learn that a curb is a kind of boundary that it is not allowed to cross without you saying "Go ahead." From the point of view of the safety of your dog as well as that of other road-users, this is certainly a valuable lesson.

This dog has learned to "Stay down" and not to stand up until its owner has said "Go ahead."

The command "Lie down"

Teach this command to your dog when it is already in a sitting position. Hold a nice treat in your hand and keep your fist closed in front of its nose to make it pick up the smell. Then move your fist down slowly and say the command "Lie down" at the same time. Interested as it is in the tidbit, your pup will follow your fist. If you then push lightly on its shoulders using your free hand, your dog will quickly understand the intention. The closer the pup comes to the floor, the more you open your hand. When it is finally lying down, you open your hand completely to enable it to get the treat.

The command "Stay"

The intention of the command "Stay" is that your dog will stand, lie, or sit in the same place as it was at the moment you gave the command. It is best to teach your dog this while it is sitting. Put your dog on the leash and let it sit down to the left of you. Then give it the command "Stay"—you may hold your hand up with the palm facing the dog—and wait a few seconds. If your pup remains sitting, then reward it immediately. If your dog understands this you can move a little farther away. Allow the leash to trail. If it remains in a sitting position then of course reward it enthusiastically. If it rises or walks toward you, say "No!" very clearly and put it back exactly in the starting position. Continue by repeating the command and then stepping back. With this command it is very important that you do not expect too much from your puppy. If it stays sitting for just a single second, immediately change the command by saying "Let go" or "Go ahead." You cannot yet expect it to stay motionless for five minutes. If you do expect this then the chances are that your dog will change the command itself. Only when your puppy understands the command really well and acts upon it are you ready to make variations on it. You may practice the command with the leash off, extend the period, or hide yourself briefly. Do not use "Stay," however, if your dog is in its place (i.e. basket or crate), as there it can decide for itself whether it is going to lie down, stand up, or bite its chewing bone.

At the command "Stay" the dog should stay, lie, or sit motionless in the same place.

Walking at leisure

If you wish to go for pleasant and relaxed walks with your Golden Retriever on its leash, it is important that you teach your dog that it may not pull on the leash. You teach it by pulling the leash briefly but noticeably whenever it pulls while you say "Bad dog!" or "No!" in a low-pitched voice. Be very consistent in so doing. You will not achieve good results if you sometimes correct your dog and sometimes do not. If your Golden Retriever is very strong and your corrections do not impress it, you might consider buying a Halti or a Gentle Leader. These "dog halters" are not put round the neck but round the head. The working of both these devices is based on the same principle. When your dog pulls the leash, the Halti will automatically exert unpleasant pressure on the nose bridge and at the same time pull the head down and sideways. In this way you can easily and effortlessly control your dog during a walk. If your dog does not pull, it will not experience any inconvenience, and thus it will get out of the habit of pulling.

A fine retrieve

10 GROOMING

Necessities

Basket or crate

You have already seen in great detail in Chapter 5 how useful a crate is. There are many different kinds of basket on the market, ranging from bags filled with polystyrene pellets to lie on, to cane baskets and dog stretchers. The best you can purchase for your pup is a plastic basket. This kind of basket is much less of an invitation to chew. Soft baskets, such as bags to lie on and cane baskets, are often torn apart by adventurous young pups. Once your dog has experienced how much fun this game is, the chances are that it will start all over again with a new basket. You can place a blanket in the basket or crate, which you should shake out every day and wash regularly. It is an advantage for this blanket to be taken along if you pay someone a visit, thereby providing the dog with its own proper place. For a grown up dog, you can safely buy a bag to lie on or a soft basket.

A cane basket and a bag to lie on

Collars and leashes

Never purchase a collar that allows for growth, preferably buy a new collar that fits correctly. A collar that is too large may give your dog an opportunity to escape. You can choose

Right: After its first birthday a Golden Retriever will usually not grow very much more.

between a collar made of good quality leather or nylon. The advantage of nylon collars is that they are almost indestructible and easy to wash. When you start training an immature dog, a choke leash will be more suitable since you cannot correct your dog using an ordinary leash.

Choke chains should be removed after training. Such a chain might get stuck and endanger your dog. Besides, a

Dog collars made of all kinds of materials and in all colors can be purchased

chain damages the dog's coat.

The best you can do is to purchase two different leashes. Buy a leash about five feet in length made from good quality leather or nylon. Purchase also a reel leash; this comes in handy when you want to give your dog more freedom to move about while you are walking.

Feeding and drinking bowls
There are many different kinds of feeding and drinking bowls on the market. They are usually made from stainless steel, plastic, or glazed ceramic. Although glazed ceramic looks fine, these bowls are not very practical for daily use as they break easily. Plastic bowls are available in various qualities. The cheaper ones are quite light in weight, which causes them to slide about the floor easily. They also quickly start to look ugly. A heavier plastic bowl does not have these disadvantages. In the long run stainless steel feeding and drinking bowls are the most suitable. They are unbreakable, easy to clean, and will last for a dog's lifetime or longer. In order to prevent these bowls from sliding, special types can be bought so that the height can be adjusted to the size of the dog.

Feeding bowls in a height-adjustable standard

Body care and health

Nails

Many people underestimate the importance of short nails. Long nails not only look ugly, they also break easily. A dog with long nails develops an awkward walk, while they also have an adverse effect on the paws, since the length of the nails makes it impossible to walk and stand normally. It is never too early to start cutting nails, for the living parts of the nails grow as well. If you leave the nails to grow it will become impossible after a while to cut them without causing pain and making them bleed. Always use a good quality nail-cutter that has been especially designed for use with dogs. Do not forget the dew claws. They are hidden in the hair just above the paw. If you do not like the idea of having to cut nails, go to a grooming parlor that will do it for you.

Teeth

Puppies have milk teeth that are replaced by adult teeth between the fourth and sixth months. During the transition period a pup may have less appetite and it will want to chew more often. During this stage some extra chewing material will be very welcome. Check the teeth at times for milk teeth that are stuck and impair the arrival of an adult tooth or molar, since this may cause the permanent teeth and molars to grow crooked. Make it a habit to check the teeth and molars of a mature dog once a month, especially those at the back. Tartar is not only the cause of bad breath—it will eventually cause periodontitis and loss of teeth. Surface dirt can be removed using a toothbrush and children's toothpaste. The actual tartar can only be removed under an anesthetic by a veterinarian. Development of tartar can be avoided by providing the dog with durable chewing bones.

Always keep the nails short.

Left: The teeth of a mature Golden Retriever

Right: There are many kinds of chewing material available.

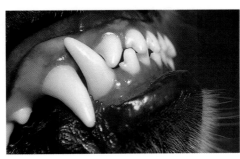

Ears

Golden Retrievers have pendulous ears and a thick coat. If you never cut away the excessive hair around the auditory duct under the earflap, it may start to get inflamed and become a source of infection. This is why you should regularly cut away the excess hair growth or ask the grooming parlor to do it for you. Check the auditory duct for dirt and excessive earwax once a week. You can clean the ears using a special cleaning agent for dogs. The dirt and earwax can be removed using a soft tissue. Since the auditory duct of dogs is not straight but runs at an angle, cotton swabs are unsuitable. Cotton swabs would just push the dirt farther inside the duct, thereby creating the risk of infection in the deeper parts of it. If your dog scratches its ears and exhibits a dark grainy and smelly secretion, it is suffering from ear mites. A veterinarian can cure this easily.

Eyes

Generally speaking, the eyes of a Golden Retriever do not need much care. However, if your Golden Retriever suffers a great deal from weeping eyes, ask your veterinarian to check for obstructed tear glands and entropion. In case of the latter (inherited) disorder one or both eyelids are pulled inward. Entropion can be cured by surgery.

Alternating nose

A very well-known phenomenon among Golden Retrievers is the so-called alternating nose. It refers to the normally black nose becoming pink in color. Discoloring of the pigment usually occurs when bitches are in season, and in both sexes also during the winter. Older Golden Retrievers almost always have a lighter-colored nose. An alternating nose is a perfectly normal and harmless phenomenon.

Fleas

Fleas are a persistent torment that can make life hard for your dog. Some Golden Retrievers are hardly bothered by their parasites, whereas after a single flea bite dogs that are allergic to fleas scratch and bite themselves until they lose their hair. If you want to solve the flea problem effectively, you will have to fight them on several fronts. Using a good quality anti-flea spray or a powder you can treat both your dog and other pets. Carpets, dog basket, chinks and cracks, at home as well as in the car, should be treated with an ambient spray. Furthermore, it is advisable to vacuum-clean everywhere, as this will remove the sources of nutrition for the flea larvae. Using a wet mop, on the other hand, is useless, as fleas just love the humidity and the warmth and are also resistant to cleaning agents. There is a new remedy on the market nowadays, which is mixed with the dogs' food.

It makes any flea that drinks the dogs' blood become sterile, thereby preventing reproduction. If you apply such an agent consistently it will work perfectly. However, due to the extended chance of re-infection you will also have to rely on conventional methods. Puppies are vulnerable and very sensitive with regard to aggressive anti-flea agents. Therefore, if you are dealing with a puppy rather than an adult dog, it is better to purchase special-purpose medicines from your veterinarian.

Ticks

Ticks are tiny parasites that dwell in bushes and long grass awaiting a hairy passer-by such as your dog to serve as a host. They fix themselves firmly into the skin and suck blood. Completely filled with blood they look like round gray warts in the hair. Ticks can be a vector for the feared

Lyme disease, which can also be dangerous for humans. A remedy against tick bites—such as an anti-tick collar—is not a luxury. Combined remedies also exist that are effective against both ticks and fleas. If your dog carries a tick, remove it preferably with the help of a special tick remover, using a turning movement. If you just pull a tick out, the jaws will remain in the skin, possibly causing an infection later.

Worms

All pups are born with roundworm infection, irrespective of whether the mother-dog was treated for worms or not. The breeder therefore will have already treated the pups several times before you take the pup home. How often you have to treat your puppy for worms depends on the kind of agent used. Therefore always ask your breeder which agent he or she has used to treat the pup, and how often and when the treatment should be repeated. A worm infection is not without risk, especially if it is neglected. Another worm that occurs often in dogs is tapeworm. You will usually discover a tapeworm infection by noticing grainy particles in

the dog's excrement or in the hair round its anus. Fleas play the role of temporary hosts for tapeworms. If your dog has fleas then there is a chance that it also has a tapeworm infection. For adult dogs, an effective anti-tapeworm treatment applied twice a year will usually be sufficient.

In tall grass and bushes your dog may pick up ticks.

Vaccinations
There are a number of life-threatening diseases against which your dog can be protected by vaccinations. The most common of these diseases are parvo, canine distemper, hepatitis, Weil's disease, and less severe leptospirosis. The vaccinations cannot all be given at the same time, but are spread out over a period of four to six weeks. A puppy's last vaccination will take place around the twelfth week. Until that time the pup is not fully protected against these diseases. In order to prevent contamination you will have to avoid places that are visited by many dogs until the vet says it is safe to go there. If you regularly take your dog to shows or leave it in kennels, a vaccination or nose drops against canine cough is not a luxury. Canine cough is highly contagious and is transmitted in places where there are many dogs and where there is a lot of barking. Many kennels have made this vaccination mandatory in addition to the other vaccinations. A vaccination against rabies is compulsory in some states and counties, and in many other countries. This vaccination has to be given at least one month beforehand and within the last year. Some vaccines are only valid for six months. At the time of the vaccination your veterinarian will provide you with a certificate that serves as proof of vac-

cination and which may be shown to the customs officers on request if traveling to another country.

Caring for the coat

Daily care
Golden Retrievers have a weather-resistant coat that also repels dirt. A Golden Retriever that has got itself dirty does not have to be washed with dog shampoo immediately. It is often sufficient to let the coat dry and brush it out subsequently. Once every so often you will however have to wash your dog. When you do, always use a special dog shampoo. A good dog shampoo does not damage the skin's oil layer.

Weil's disease is commonly transmitted through rat urine. The more often your dog swims, the higher the risk of contamination

If you wish your Golden Retriever to always look nice and tidy, you will have to thoroughly brush its coat down to the skin every other day. Depending on the density of its hair, a Golden Retriever may need to be trimmed at a professional dog-trimming parlor. You can learn to trim your dog yourself with the help of the following step-by-step instructional pictures. Show trimming, however, demands a little more. If you want to learn this it is best for you to start training with someone experienced in showing Golden Retrievers.

Step by step

1 This Golden Retriever female with her heavy coat desperately needs a thorough brush and trim.

2 Tangles are found particularly in the very hairy hindquarters. This part has to be combed thoroughly every other day. Existing tangles should be clipped away.

3 Subsequently, brush the hair thoroughly down to the skin.

4 Trim the tail hair into shape. Do not forget to brush and comb it first.

5 Hold the tail in a horizontal position and cut away the excess hair in one fluent movement from the tip to the root. The tail has to taper off in the direction of the tip.

6 Continue by holding the tail in a vertical position and cut off the ends of the hairs.

7 Small stones, twigs and so on may get stuck in the hair between the pads. Excess hair may also lead to an impaired foot position. Cut off the excess hair using a sharp pair of scissors; also between the pads.

8 Lay the dog on its side with the back part of its hind legs toward you. In this way you can cut away the long hair at the back of the leg from the hock to the paw. Preferably use notched thinning scissors.

9 Cut the hair of the foreleg in the same manner, but start in this case from the wrist joint.

10 Carefully cut away the hairs hanging over the earflap, thus following the rim of the ear. Here also the use of notched thinning scissors is best.

11 Too much hair on the earflap should be thinned using notched thinning scissors.

12 The long hairs that grow beneath the ear, round the auditory duct, and the root of the ear should also be kept short in order to give the ear some air.

13 Cut and thin out the long hair beneath the ear and on the neck. For a good result, again use the notched thinning scissors.

14 Thin out the hair on the neck down to the breastbone. You should also cut short the hair sticking out from the breastbone and surrounding area.

15 The longer hair at the back of the neck is also thinned using notched thinning scissors.

16 The long hairs on the forelegs (the feathering) are a natural feature of the Golden Retriever. You might trim them a little to make them look tidier.

17 The same goes for the hair on the belly. Be careful not to cut away too much.

18 Brush the hair on the hind legs thoroughly. Cut away the hair overlapping the hock, using notched thinning scissors.

After a thorough trim and brush this friendly bitch looks neat and tidy

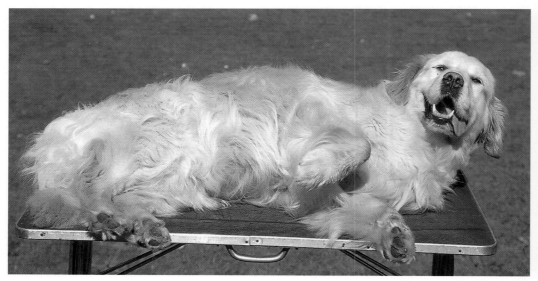

You will find it more convenient — and also better for your back — to teach the dog to lie on a table or some other raised and stable place during grooming. Use a rubber mat as the surface to lie on in order to prevent slipping.

11 FEEDING

Instant dog food

Instant dog foods of the best quality contain everything that your dog needs. It is unnecessary and sometimes even harmful to your dog's health to add supplementary nutrients to the whole food. This is especially true of calcium—this used to be added to the food of pups of larger-sized breeds in earlier days, as people assumed that it would be beneficial to bone growth. This actually caused much too high an intake of calcium in these dogs, where the calcium was subsequently deposited on the bones and joints. Many of these dogs acquired chronic physical problems as a result of this. Excessive protein is just as unhealthy, as this will stimulate

Dry dog food

Right: When given sufficient physical exercise and specially adapted food, even older Golden Retrievers will stay on top form.

unbalanced rapid growth. This may lead to problems with the joints and may cause your dog growing pains.

Here are just a few reasons why you should not mix meat or canned food with instant dry food for your dog. It is a known fact that some nutrients may have an adverse affect

on each other when mixed in the wrong proportions. Therefore it is important that your dog receives the nutrients that it needs not only in the right quantities, but also in the correct proportions of nutrients, vitamins, and minerals. Good brands of dog food contain the correct ratios, and you will certainly not deprive your dog of proper feeding if you choose one quality-brand whole dog food and stay with it. But once a week you might for a change give your dog some meat, such as tripe and heart, instead of its instant food. It will be beneficial to your dog's intestinal flora. It would be ideal if your dog loves to eat the food that you have chosen, but this is certainly not a guarantee of quality. If dogs are allowed to choose, they will prefer fat and salty food, and everybody knows that too much of this is unhealthy.

Diner

Dinner

Canned food, mixer, and meat
Not all kinds of dog food are complete in themselves. Some canned food and other kinds of frozen food such as chicken, headcheese, and tripe are incomplete, although whole deep-frozen and canned foods do exist. Incomplete canned food and meat should be blended with a "mixer," if you supply them every day. A mixer is a dinner or a flake food that does not contain dried meat. The proportions you should use are indicated on the mixer packaging. Although fresh meat is without question healthy for a dog and comes

as near its natural nutritional needs as possible, you will have to be careful about using fresh pork.

This meat may be contaminated with Aujeszky's disease, which can be fatal for dogs. Dogs that come into contact with pigs are also exposed to an increased risk. Vaccinations against Aujeszky's disease are available, but they unfortunately do not offer complete protection.

Quantities

Pups have a small stomach and should therefore be given four to five small meals a day. Later on, the portions may be increased and the number reduced to two meals. Adult dogs are best fed twice a day. The body utilizes smaller meals better and they put less stress on the digestive system. There are no rules for the quantity of food a dog needs, as the quantity not only depends on the brand and the kind of food, but also differs from one breed to another and between individual dogs. Hence it might very well be that the amount of food your dog needs differs from the guidelines on the package.

Too fat or too thin

Adult Golden Retrievers weigh between 60 and 73 lbs (27 and 33 kg). Only a few dogs are too thin; most are overweight. There may be a medical cause for being overweight, but the reason is usually too much food in combination with too little physical exercise. Being over-

Active and working dogs need more food than dogs that get little exercise.

weight is very unhealthy and paves the way for health problems. A dog that is too fat will benefit from more exercise and a reduced daily food intake. Green beans will not make a dog fat, but they do stop the craving for food. You may give this vegetable without a problem if your dog continues to stare and beg from its barely filled feeding bowl. If you are in doubt whether your dog is overweight, ask your veterinarian for advice. Sometimes dogs reject food. If they are otherwise sound and healthy then this is probably because they are being spoiled. The dog probably has learned that its owner will quickly serve it a tidbit if it does not touch its dried food. In such cases a day of fasting will certainly not harm the animal. During teeth change,

A regular chew on a chewy bone will prevent the dog from developing tooth tartar or worse

between the fourth and the sixth months, dogs usually have less appetite. This is also perfectly harmless. Food rejection may however also have a medical cause, such as toothache, fever, or a foreign object in its stomach. If you are anxious about it, you should seek advice from a veterinarian.

Physical condition

Though nowadays poor food hardly exists any more, not all kinds of food are suitable for just any kind of dog. Whether the food you give is not suitable, or is no longer suitable, can be detected for example from a change in the

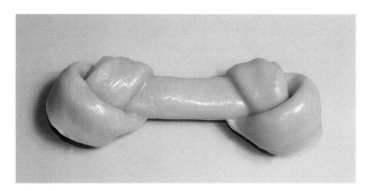

A plastic chewy bone

consistency or color of the dog's stool, a general deterioration in its physical condition, or dandruff and loss of hair. If you observe one of these symptoms, you will have to take your dog to the veterinarian for a checkup. If no physical cause can be detected, a different kind or another brand of food might be the solution. Never on the other hand completely change the food for your dog overnight, as this may produce diarrhea. It is better to mix a daily increasing quantity of the new food with the food that your dog is used to. A change of food may lead to improvement only after many months.

Things to chew on

In order to prevent tooth tartar and decay, your dog must use its teeth on a regular basis. Chewing is also a good remedy for boredom, which for certain dogs might end up with them biting your personal belongings to pieces.

Bones made from pressed buffalo hide and large boiled cow bones are ideal. Ground cowhide (in the form of sticks for munching) and other soft chewing articles such as tripe rolls are tasty snacks but contribute little, if at all, to the cleaning of the teeth. Preferably do not give the bones of poultry, pigs, or game. These bones may splinter and subsequently damage the intestines of your dog. Marrowbones can also be dangerous—they have more than once got stuck like a rock around the lower jaws of dogs. A safe and durable alternative for the chews that are made from animal offal is plastic chewing knuckles. These have the same effect as traditional knuckle bones but are more durable and hygienic.

12 PHYSICAL EXERCISE AND ACTIVITIES

Physical exercise

During its first year of life a Golden Retriever pup will grow tremendously. This growth will put a heavy burden on the bones, the joint attachments and the ligaments. It is therefore important that you ensure your dog has the opportunity to develop a sound skeleton. Hip and elbow dysplasia, for instance, are partly hereditary, but food and exercise—especially during the first year—also have a pronounced impact. If during this period your dog's skeleton is put under too much pressure, if the pressure is unbalanced or exerted for too long a time, problems may develop that will last for the dog's entire life. Walking up or down stairs, playing with dogs that are much bigger and stronger, and jumping up from a slippery house floor all inhibit optimal development. It is better to take the puppy

During the growing period, try as much as possible to avoid jumping and other movements that put pressure on the joints

Right: Car sickness often has to do with nervousness and anxiety. By making short trips to places that are fun for the dog, carsickness can be prevented or cured

for several short walks each day and avoid unnecessarily complicated movements.

In addition to controlled regular physical exercise, one should also keep an eye on the weight of the growing dog. In order to put as little pressure as possible on the joints it is important that it does not become overweight as it matures.

In the car

Safety issues
You will regularly transport your dog by car. In these cases, an indoor kennel or crate that you can put in a car or a safety harness that you can use to attach your dog to the back seat are ideal. If you have a van, the cargo space would be the proper place for it. Preferably attach a special car rack or netting in between the cargo space and the passenger area. You should preferably not transport the dog unattached on the back seat or sitting next to the driver. You might be impeded while driving, and your dog will not have any protection at all if you have an accident.

Car sickness
You can prevent your dog from getting car-sick by not feeding it immediately before you leave. When you make a long journey by car it is sensible to make regular stops and give your dog the opportunity to urinate and to walk a little. Many dogs that vomit and suffer from nausea are actually afraid of car journeys. If for instance you only transport your dog by car when you take it to the veterinarian or to the kennels, it will link driving to something negative. By taking your dog out for a regular short drive, with something enjoyable waiting for it at the end, such as a walk through the woods, you can help your dog overcome its fear. Get your puppy accustomed to short drives while it is not yet vulnerable to carsickness. In this case too make sure that there is something enjoyable waiting at the end of the drive. In this way you will ensure that your dog will not start to hate car journeys. If however your dog keeps on being car-sick, your veterinarian can provide you with a treatment for it.

Swimming
Swimming is the ideal physical exercise for a Golden Retriever. They love everything wet and they are eager to retrieve objects from the water. In better pet shops and at dog shows you can buy special retrieval dummies that will float. Such dummies do cost money of course, but they are certainly safer than a branch or a stick. When the weather is

hot you cannot do your Golden Retriever a greater favor than allowing it to swim and to retrieve. But even when the weather is less favorable the dog will love to get into the water. In the latter case always take a large towel with you to dry the dog. Once you are back home, you should not let it dry outdoors or in a drafty place. This could make a Golden Retriever ill. Be careful about where you allow your dog to swim. Treacherous undercurrents, bacteria that cause diseases, fishing nets, steep banks and long stringy water plants are not only dangerous to human beings but also to dogs.

Games

Retrieving

You will notice that your Golden Retriever as a puppy already adores carrying objects in its mouth. Subsequently you can teach it to bring these objects to you. When your pup is carrying something in its mouth, then call it by name and say "Fetch it!" in a cheerful tone. By making inviting gestures while squatting down, and by encouraging your dog with your voice, you will quickly make it understand what you want it to do. Reward it enthusiastically when it has brought you the object and exchange it for a tidbit, or throw it away once more. When your pup drags your new shoes or your eyeglasses around, do not get angry. Let it retrieve the

Swimming—an occupation much cherished by many Golden Retrievers

object and exchange it for something it is allowed to have. You cannot expect anything else from a young pup than for it to bring an object to you and release it immediately. Later on you can teach it to sit in front of you and to release the object only after you have given the command "Let go!" You may then teach it to stay sitting next to you until the object touches the ground and to move only after you have given the command "Retrieve!" What is true of retrieving from water is also true of retrieving on land: sticks and branches are usually not safe. Preferably use a retrieval block or a soft dummy.

Tracking games

Golden Retrievers have a keen sense of smell and they love to use it. This is why they adore tracking games. Tracking

What is learned in the cradle lasts forever.

demands much of their energy and concentration. The effort that your dog makes when it tracks down an object should therefore not be underestimated. Various sorts of tracking games may be invented. You may for instance hide its favorite toy under a bucket, and then let your dog search for it. In the beginning, you should not make it too difficult. Your dog first has to understand what the intention of the game is. When your dog realizes what you expect it to do, you can hide several balls, out of which your dog has to find its own ball. You may also suspend several cloths from a low clothesline. Two cloths you have had in one of your pants pockets for a while, so that they will have attracted a scent specific enough to be discerned by your dog. One of these cloths you hang on the clothesline between some "neutral" cloths, e.g. clothes that have just been laundered. Let the Golden Retriever sniff at the cloth that you still have in your pocket and let it search for the other one with the same scent. The command that you can use is "Seek!" It goes without saying that you should let it search on its

Dummies come in various sizes, materials, and colors.

own, without any help. Do not forget to lavish praise on your dog when it has found the correct piece of cloth.

Hunting training sessions and obedience contests

Your Golden Retriever is a multipurpose dog that will stand out in both hunting training sessions and games of obedience and skill. Should you be interested in these kinds of dog sports, then it is important to start as soon as possible by joining a club. It is better not to teach your dog your own set of commands as it will be very difficult to change these later on. The commands used in these training sessions may be entirely different from the ones you have taught your dog, while the exercises sometimes have to be carried out differently as well. By becoming a member of an association where these kinds of sport are practiced, you can save yourself and your dog a lot of time and trouble.

Let your dog find its favorite ball during tracking games.

13 Diseases and Defects

J.W.H.M. Strikkers, veterinarian

How do you know when your dog is ill?

In order to find out whether your pet is ill, it is important to be well acquainted with its ordinary behavior. When your dog is healthy, how much appetite does it have, and what is its stool like? How much does it drink, how much does it urinate, and how does it behave? When you observe something abnormal, you will first have to measure the dog's temperature (rectally). The normal temperature of a dog at rest is 99.5–101.3 degrees Fahrenheit (37.5–38.5 degrees Celsius). If its temperature is outside this range, or if the dog suffers from severe diarrhea or vomits regularly, you should contact a veterinarian.

Dogs that are ill are usually listless

Uteritis

Uteritis is a common problem among bitches of four years and older, irrespective of the breed. The illness usually starts some four to eight weeks after the dog's season or after it has received an injection to prevent it getting into season. The illness is usually marked by drowsy behavior, extreme thirst, and sometimes a cloudy secretion from the vulva. Usually a case of uteritis that occurs after the season cannot be treated with antibiotics. This is because in most cases there is not only a bacterial infection but also a dete-

Right: Do not allow your dog to walk around carrying dead animals. They can make your dog ill.

rioration of the walls of the uterus. The only effective cure is to remove the uterus by surgery. If there is a delay in carrying out the operation, the bitch may die as a result.

Foreskin infection
Foreskin infection is a frequent disorder, not only among Golden Retrievers. The infection is indicated by a greenish secretion from the foreskin. Rinsing the foreskin daily using a medicinal liquid in combination with an ointment and/or a treatment with pills provides a temporary cure. In 95 percent of the cases only castration will cure the problem permanently. Infection of the foreskin is in fact harmless.

Poisoning
A dog that has been poisoned may show various symptoms depending on the kind of poison. These symptoms are vomiting, copious dribble, diarrhea, abdominal cramps, and shivering. Sometimes the dog has dry spots on its skin, or it may go into a coma. In order to save the dog it is not only important to seek advice from a veterinarian quickly, but also to find out what kind of poison it has swallowed. If possible, take the container or package with you to the veterinarian. Some poisons can be eliminated by inducing vomiting, but in the case of other substances, such as paint thinner or gasoline, it is actually better not to do this. In such cases you can provide the animal with milk, Norit (activated carbon), or raw eggs in order to prevent the poisonous substances from being absorbed by the body.

Anal gland overfilling

The anal glands of a dog are situated to the left and right of the anus about half an inch deep. If your dog is bothered by these glands, it will try to bite itself in these places, or it will try to relieve the itching by scraping its bottom over the ground. A veterinarian can squeeze out the contents of the glands, and this will give immediate relief. If there are repeated attacks it is advisable to remove the glands by surgery.

Hip dysplasia

Hip dysplasia (HD) is a frequent disorder, predominantly among breeds of larger dogs such as the Golden Retriever. HD is a generic name for developing disorders of the hip joints, which are determined by both hereditary and external factors. In dogs that suffer from HD the hip joints undergo an irreversible and aggravating change. This change is marked by a weakening of the joint capsule, and swelling, weakening and rupture of part of the ligaments. There is also an abnormal development of the head of the thighbone and the hip socket. The joint cartilage is affected as well, resulting in an uncontrolled growth at the location of the joint (arthritis). Dogs that are affected by this disorder have trouble getting on their feet and/or walking, they have less stamina and sometimes show a one-sided alternating lameness. Overextension of the hips may be very painful. There is no real cure for HD, and therefore complete recovery is not possible. Through balanced nutrition, proper exercise of the muscles in which most of the dog's movements are made in a straight line, and by avoiding obesity, you may reduce the chances of HD developing. You can only know if your dog really has HD anyway when you have X-rays taken. Nobody can diagnose HD from the way the dog walks or lies down; you can only suspect it. If

You cannot see whether a dog has hip dysplasia from the way it lies down or moves

HD is diagnosed when your dog is still young, tilting the pelvis through a surgical operation gives good prospects of recovery. The pelvis is tilted over the head of the hip in order to allow the hip joint to perform its normal function without excessive wear of the hip joint. This operation is, however, expensive and is performed in specialized animal clinics. You can also opt for painkillers, muscle strengtheners, and controlled exercise. Homeopathic treatment and acupuncture may also provide some relief. Owners try to fight this disease by ensuring that breeding is with animals that have been officially tested for HD and have proved to be free of it.

Elbow dysplasia

Elbow dysplasia (ED) is a generic name for a group of disorders of the elbow with more or less a common cause, i.e. an unbalanced growth of the radius and the ulna, and/or development disorders in the bones surrounding the elbow joint. The cause is hereditary and is also determined by such factors as nutrition, exercise, and weight. Under ED are classed UAP (ununited anconeal process) and FCP (fragmented coronoid process). Both disorders indicate a loose fragment of the ulna, while the different names refer to the exact location of the dis-

By only breeding with healthy dogs, hereditary disorders can be controlled in the long run.

order. Another well-known disorder is OCD (Osteochondritis dessicans), referring to a loose piece of cartilage in the upper elbow. An "incongruous" elbow joint means that the elbow joint is poorly connected. FCP, OCD, and incongruence of the elbow joint in particular are relatively common among Golden Retrievers. The characteristics of all three of these disorders are more or less the same. One or both of the dog's forelegs is crippled, they have difficulty standing and do not want to walk much or at all. Overextension of the elbow joints is painful and the elbows may be overfilled. Making the correct diagnosis is very important with respect to the treatment. This could be the removal of loose fragments from the elbow joint through surgery, surgical correction of the length of the ulna, or rest in combination with inflammation-suppressing medicines. The sooner a diagnosis is made, the better the prospects are for the dog., Prevention of these disorders in the Golden Retriever is attempted by taking X-rays of dogs that are used for breeding.

Progressive retina atrophy

Progressive retina atrophy, PRA for short, is a disorder of the retina. In this case a reduction in the number of retinal cones is apparent, with night blindness as a result. If the decay of the retina continues the rods will also be affected, eventually leading to total blindness when the Golden Retriever has reached the age of five to nine years. This disorder cannot be treated. As it is clear that the disorder is inherited, using animals that suffer from this disorder for breeding is not recommended. Breeding animals are therefore checked for this disorder every year.

Special tests for the detection of eye disorders have been developed

Cataract

Cataract is the term for the partial or complete whitening of the lens. This causes the animal's eyesight to be more or less impaired. In the case of complete whitening the dog will be unable to see anything at all and treatment will be necessary. The only cure for cataract is an operation in which the lens is removed and replaced by an artificial lens. Golden Retrievers are born with a kind of cataract, meaning that the disorder is already apparent while the dog is still young. Old age cataract also occurs in Golden Retrievers. This usually starts at the age of five to six years and usually worsens with age.

Epilepsy

Epilepsy is characterized by uncontrolled movements of the body, or parts of the body, in which the dog may become unconscious. Epilepsy refers not only to falling over and convulsions, which are well known, but also the cases in which the dog shakes its head for several minutes or those in which its foreleg shivers continuously. This has to do with the disorderly "discharging" of the brain's nerve cells. During a heavy attack, the brain will completely "discharge" in a certain rhythm. In case of a focal (partial) epilepsy the discharge will occur in a certain part of the brain. Epilepsy usually starts in the brain (primary epilepsy), but it is also possible that a metabolic disorder will irritate the brain thereby triggering secondary epilepsy. In the case of primary epilepsy the first symptoms occur around the age of 12 to 18 months; at first the attacks are short (lasting some two to five minutes) and the level of occurrence is low (once a fortnight). Usually the seriousness and the frequency increase, and the attacks start to occur in clusters; e.g. five in 24 hours and then nothing for a period of two weeks. If your Golden Retriever starts to get epileptic attacks, your vet will first try to find out through blood tests, for instance, whether there is any question of secondary epilepsy. If your dog has primary epilepsy, it will be treated with drugs. This treatment will last throughout its lifetime, with varying results.

Food allergy

A dog that has a food allergy usually suffers from itching all over its body, sometimes with pimples in the groin, in the pits of the forelegs, and on the stomach. The feces may vary in consistency. Food allergy is caused by certain food components. This may be a chemical preserving or coloring agent in the food, but also certain proteins such as those found in pork, beef, and fish can cause allergic reactions. In the first case you should give your dog food without chemical additives. In the second case you should resort to feeding only lamb to your dog, as this causes allergy in very few dogs. Do not give your dog anything else to eat, so as to exclude the intake of certain proteins.

Atopy

Atopy is caused by an allergic reaction of the body to compounds (allergens) that have been breathed in. The external symptoms, such as biting and licking its legs, scraping its head across the floor, and scratching the pits of foreleg and groin, are caused by the allergic reactions that the allergens induce. Allergens might be for instance house mites, tree and grass pollen, and scales from the dead skin of cats, dogs, and humans. The first indications of atopy become apparent between the sixth month and the third year. An allergy test will show which allergens produce the strongest reaction in your dog. The best thing to do is to avoid as far as possible any contact between your dog and these allergens. In the case of an allergy produced by household dust or house mites this will mean that you will have to vacuum-clean frequently and preferably not have carpets. Comb and brush the dog regularly. When you

Dogs can be allergic to many compounds, for instance grass pollen.

wash your dog, use a mild medicinal shampoo. Nutritious food is also very essential. This food has to contain sufficient building materials for the skin and the coat. Adding specific fatty acids to the food in the form of a dermatological oil may also help.

Hot spot

Hot spots, otherwise known as rashes, develop because of the dog biting its skin. Hot spots frequently occur among Golden Retrievers. A flea bite, but equally any small irritation as a result of shedding, may be the cause. The dog starts to scratch and to lick, the skin becomes moist causing the undercoat to stick together, and the underlying skin becomes inflamed. This will then cause extra irritation, as a result of which the dog will start to scratch even harder, and so on. Clean the spot twice a day using shampoo containing Betadine as well as an anti-inflammatory ointment.

Itching

Atopy, hot spots, and a food allergy are not the only things to cause itching and inconvenience. Dogs may be allergic to flea saliva, in which case a single bite by a flea will be enough to cause an allergic reaction. Mites may also be the

This hot spot just above the ear is already getting better.

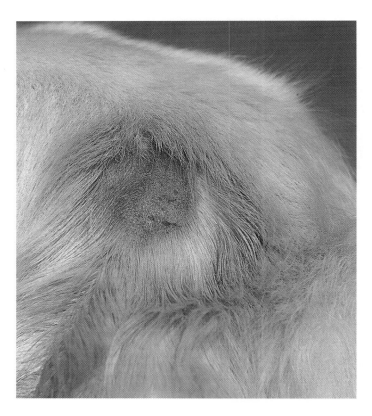

cause of problems. Mites cannot be seen with the naked eye, but the vet may discover these parasites with the use of special equipment.

Canine cough

Canine cough (or kennel cough) is a very contagious affection , which is caused by the bacteria called Bordetella bronchoseptica. This affection is characterized by a continuous and severe cough, sometimes accompanied by a tendency to vomit. Adult dogs do not always appear to be ill when they have canine cough. Pups and older dogs, since they are more vulnerable, may become very ill. This is because severe bronchitis or pneumonia has developed from the initial illness. Canine cough is treated with antibiotics and cough-suppressing drugs. Obviously prevention is better than cure, so have your dog vaccinated. The proper vaccination is the so-called "nose-drops vaccination," whereby live but weakened bacteria are placed in the dog's nose, thus providing it with protection for at least six months.

Canine cough is contracted in places where there are many dogs together and where there is a lot of barking, such as kennels and dog shows.

14 BREEDING

Preliminary considerations

Your family situation

Although a litter of puppies is fun and "cute," it actually has less romantic features also. Golden Retrievers have large litters. You may expect six to eight puppies on aver-

age, but there might be even more. Pups are not only cute. They can also make a lot of noise and produce a lot of urine and feces. They are playful and spontaneous, and occasionally do not leave your furniture and plants in one piece. Your bitch's offspring will determine everything you do at home for two months at least. Not everyone is capable of caring for and looking after a bitch and her pups. It demands much dedication, time, and devotion.

Financial aspects

The whole enterprise of breeding can become rather expensive. Consider for instance the stud fee, travel expenses, pedigree requests, vaccinations, worming, adaptations to the interior of your home, and food. Something may go wrong, in which case a veterinarian will be needed, which is often quite expensive. Therefore never engage in breeding as a way of making money. On the contrary, make sure that you have considerable financial reserves.

The bitch

The mother-to-be must have a friendly and stable character. She should not be angst-ridden or show any other deviant characteristics. Apart from the fact that these features could be hereditary, an unstable mother does not set a good example for her pups, which of course copy a lot from their mother. Ideally she will have proved her will-

Far right: Ask your veterinarian for medicines to worm the pups and follow the worming schedule closely.

ingness to work in the (training) field. The mother should excel in physical fitness and be a beautiful representative of her breed. This should be the opinion not just of your acquaintances but also of a canine specialist. The mother should of course be healthy and not possess any hereditary defects or allergies.

Hereditary defects

Nobody can tell from looking at a dog whether it suffers from hip and/or elbow dysplasia. Only an official X-ray sent by your veterinarian to a special commission can reveal this. This commission will carefully examine the X-rays and form an opinion about the quality of the hips. The judgment is binding and the outcome will show later on the puppies' pedigrees.

The mother-to-be should be in perfect condition.

Submit your bitch to a thorough checkup for eye disorders such as PRA. This kind of disorder occurs with this breed. You show a lack of understanding and a poor sense of responsibility if you do not submit your bitch to a checkup before it is covered, and it may also get you into trouble. If one or more pups turns out to suffer from a genetic disorder, the purchasers will have the right to hold you liable and press charges in order to receive compensation for medical or other expenses incurred. Only if you can provide official test results of both your bitch and the sire will you be able to prove that you have done your best to breed healthy pups. If such is the case then you cannot be blamed. Remember however that a bitch can also transmit more than is actually visible. Even though your bitch has been declared without fault, she can still transmit a genetic disorder from her parents or ancestors to her offspring. Research into the animal's pedigree is certainly not a luxury.

The breeding

The sire
Everything is ready. Your bitch has passed all her tests with honor and there might already be people interested in the pups. Now it is important to find a proper sire. You can go to shows and in particular championship club matches to watch stud-dogs. If you are a member of your dog's breed society—which certainly is recommended—you can ask for the addresses of stud-dog owners. Please bear in mind that the stud-dog should be at least of the same quality as your bitch. Be aware also that two best-quality dogs do not necessarily produce top-quality pups; the two might simply not go along with each other very well. If you are on good terms with the breeder of your dog, ask for his or her advice and ask the stud-dog's owner too. The breed society may also provide assistance.

The time for covering
A bitch is usually covered during her third or fourth season, i.e. in her second year. If a bitch is covered earlier, she will not yet have reached her prime and might not be mentally mature. If you wait longer, for example until after the fourth year of her life, she will be less fertile and the chances of complications are increased. Your dog should of

The stud-dog should at least possess the same qualities as your bitch; better qualities are however preferred.

course have had all its vaccinations and she should be wormed well ahead of the covering. She should not have any fleas and should be neither too thin nor too fat. She must be in peak condition. Bitches usually are in heat for a period of three weeks in every six months. A swollen vulva and some blood loss indicate that they are on heat. The bitch is not fertile during its entire season but usually between the tenth and thirteenth day. During this period she will allow herself to be covered. It is common practice to let the bitch be covered twice, with one day for recovery in between. After the covering, the dog's penis will swell up causing the animals to remain coupled together through their sexual organs. This standing coupled together may

The bitch shows that she wants to be covered when she swings her tail aside.

last from about ten minutes to as much as 45 minutes. Sometimes a coupling does not occur but the bitch nevertheless absorbs the semen.

During the gestation
Bitches are usually with pup for a period of nine weeks, counted from the first day of the mating. During the first weeks no special precautions need yet be taken. But it goes without saying that the bitch will not benefit from too much physical effort. Take her out for a steady walk, preferably several times a day, so as to maintain her physical fitness. Never give her extra vitamins or drugs without

consulting your veterinarian first, since this could affect the development of the fetuses. If you wish to use an anti-flea agent, then again ask your veterinarian for advice first. During the first four weeks you will usually not notice any signs of pregnancy. Maybe you will notice some small change of behavior. She might for example become rather more attached to you. From about the fifth week of the gestation onward, the belly-line changes and the milk glands will swell a little. Around the sixth week, her belly really starts to thicken. If you want to know earlier whether your bitch is pregnant, take her for examination by your veterinarian on the 28th day of the gestation. It has been shown that on this day the fetuses can be touched the easiest and they will also show on an ultra-sonograph. Only from around the fifth week will your bitch need more food. As the pups occupy an increasing amount of space, your bitch will not be able to digest large amounts of food. For this reason you should give her smaller meals distributed throughout the day. Her daily ration may slowly be doubled and then reduced once the puppies start to eat.

The actual covering is very brief.

Having the litter

The whelping box
The best place for the mother dog to give birth to her pups is a special whelping box. This box will function as living

quarters for both the mother and her pups for several weeks after the birth and should therefore be made of solid material that is easy to disinfect. Both the mother and the pups are vulnerable to cold rising from the ground, which is why the box should always be slightly raised off the floor. You can use a wooden base for this. It used to be common practice to use newspapers and cloths as filling for the box, but thin corrugated paper, which you can buy by the roll, is actually much more handy and safer as well. The pups will have a much better grip and they will not get stained by newsprint. The biggest disadvantage of cloths and blankets is that the pups might get tangled up in them. You can introduce the box in the seventh week of the pregnancy.

The ideal size of a whelping box is about 3 ft 6 in (length) x 4 ft (width) x 1 ft 6 in (height).

Accessories

Well before the birth you will need to have the following things available:

- Digital thermometer
- Piles of clean towels
- Big roll of corrugated paper
- Puppy feeding bottle
- Bitch milk replacement
- Disinfectant
- Accurate kitchen scale
- Heat-radiating red lamp

Preparations

It is best to put the whelping box in a quiet place, well away from people and other animals. Many bitches will get nervous if they are disturbed in close proximity to the box, especially if they are a first time mother-to-be. The average pregnancy lasts about 63 days, i.e. nine weeks. By measuring the bitch's temperature you will be able to see when labor is about to start. Do this at the same time every day. Most bitches show a drop in temperature of one or two degrees Fahrenheit some 24 hours before they start whelping (giving birth). Many bitches will also become restless a few days before whelping. They may start digging in the box—sometimes even very energetically—and may begin doing this in the garden. If your bitch does start digging in the garden, do not leave it there alone any more. She may try to have her litter in the garden where it is certainly neither sterile nor comfortable. Every birth will be different and this book cannot cover all the possible complications. Good communication with the breeder of your bitch, the owner of the stud-dog and/or the veterinarian is very worthwhile during these difficult days. They can provide you with support by phone. Your vet's attitude is of particular importance at this time. Not every vet will be eager to pay you a visit in the middle of the night or on a weekend. It is best to be aware of this in good time so as to have the opportunity to find yourself a veterinarian with a more flexible attitude. If you are unsure of your ability to assist as a "midwife," ask somebody experienced to help you on the spot.

Birth

Giving birth starts when the bitch has had her first contraction. This contraction is noticeably different from the other contractions in its intensity. The first pup is usually born within an hour of the first contraction. The first thing you will see is the fluid-filled amniotic sac protruding from the vulva. The pup is contained in the amniotic sac and as long as this is intact the pup will have sufficient oxygen. Shortly after, the pup will be born, often with the cord still attached to the placenta. The placenta may be expelled directly after the birth of the pup, but if the cord is broken the arrival of the placenta may be postponed. Always make a note of the arrival of the placenta and check that it is complete. If the placenta or parts of it stay behind in the uterus, the bitch may become extremely ill. An experienced bitch will bite through the membranes and the cord. She will lick her offspring clean and dry, and by licking the pup thoroughly she will also start it breathing. If your bitch is rather clumsy or if it does not understand what to do, it will be you that has to cut the cords, remove the membranes, and

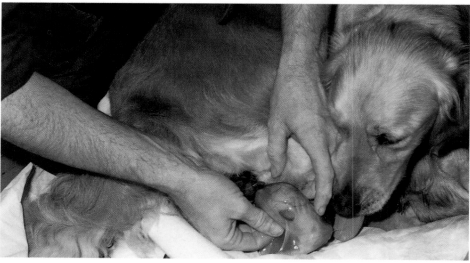

dry the pups. The most important thing is that you remove the surrounding membranes and if necessary also the mucus and fluid from the puppy's mouth and nose in order to enable it to breathe. The bitch will normally eat the placenta. If however she has more than five offspring, the large number of placentas might be just too much of a good thing and you would do better to remove any remaining. The next pup might appear almost immediately after the first one, but it might also keep you waiting for half an hour or more. If the bitch is pushing unsuccessfully for a long period of time or if she stops having contractions, you should contact your veterinarian. After the bitch has brought her last pup into the world she will usually relax. Give her some water to drink and take her with you to the garden to give her a chance to relieve herself. Meanwhile somebody else can clean and disinfect the whelping box.

Two bitches and one dog (on the left). Three excellent examples of the breed.

Marking and weighing

Golden Retriever pups all look very much alike. They do not have spots or patterns to distinguish them from the others in the litter. It is however important to follow the development and growth of each pup individually. This will give you the opportunity to intervene if the growth of one or more puppies is slow. You can mark the pups with nail polish on their toes, for example, or on the back. Weigh each puppy, make a note of the birth weight, possibly any special features, the sex, and the time of birth. Then weigh the pups subsequently every day at the same time and keep a note of your findings. Weighing is very important, as the loss of only three or four ounces is very difficult to observe otherwise.

After-care

When the birth is over, ask your veterinarian to come and check the pups and the bitch. He or she will usually give her an injection to make the uterus contract. If there is still a pup or a piece of placenta left behind, it will be forced out by the contraction that the injection induces. Keep a close eye on the bitch during the first weeks. A discharge from the vulva, red at first and later slightly pink, is absolutely normal. Take her temperature every day at the same time and watch carefully for sudden lows or highs. Keep a close eye on the milk glands as well. They should not change color or become hard. In order to prevent the pups from damaging the delicate milk glands of the mother you should cut or file their sharp nails. If the litter is born during the summer, you will not need a heat lamp; otherwise suspend a lamp above the whelping box about eight inches above your bitch's shoulder level. Leave the heat lamp switched on round the clock.

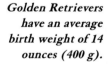

Golden Retrievers have an average birth weight of 14 ounces (400 g).

The young pups

The first weeks of life

The first weeks of a puppy's life consist of drinking and sleeping. As long as the pups do not yet receive additional food, the bitch will massage their bellies in order to stimulate defecation. She will carefully clean up the feces. If your bitch produces milk in sufficient quantities and takes good care of her pups, you will hardly hear them. If however the pups start to walk around squealing and whining or lie in a corner softly moaning, this may be an indication of a shortage of food, an ambient temperature that is too low, or some other problem. Contact your vet in such cases. Around the tenth day the eyes of the pups open, and after two to three weeks the pups will start to take their first faltering steps within the box.

Mother and pups are doing well.

Risk of infection

Pups are very susceptible to disease until they are vaccinated. Although they receive antibodies through the breast milk, these do not give total protection. Do not walk your dogs out on the street but give them the opportunity to relieve themselves in your garden. Do not allow strange dogs, or people that have a sick dog at home, to enter your home. Usually you do not have to take any extreme measures—pups are not so fragile. Do not exclude your pups from daily life because you fear the risk of infection, as it is important for their development that your pups get acquainted with ordinary things. Let them be picked up and cuddled by your children, under supervision, and do not be afraid of having the radio or TV on. These apparently insignificant things may make a world of difference during later character building.

Weeks four to six

Between the third and the fifth week puppies may be given additional food, depending on the size of the litter and the condition of your bitch. Always buy good-quality milk food for puppies. Not every pet store keeps this kind of food in stock, so order it in advance. Some breeders prefer to give their pups baby food, but puppy replacement milk is much nearer the pups' nutritional needs. When the pups are used to the replacement milk, you can slowly accustom them to puppy dry food. For the first week you should soak it in warm water. Cooked and ground red meat and cooked chicken are very suitable, but always add dry food, as meat alone does not contain sufficient nutrients. Always disinfect the feeding and drinking bowls of the pups after use. As soon as the pups start to eat by themselves the bitch will stop cleaning up their urine and feces. You will have to take over this task from her. When the pups are being bottle-fed it is also time to give them their first vaccination.

Pups that are one week old. Well fed and healthy pups sleep a lot.

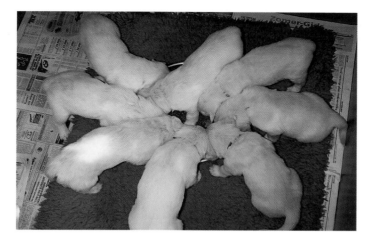

These four-week-old pups are already accustomed to food that is more substantial than mother's milk.

Weeks seven to ten

When the pups are about six to seven weeks old, most bitches will relinquish their duties as a mother. She will come with you for a walk as she used to do, although you should avoid places that are frequented by other dogs. Pups at this age almost exclusively eat dry food for pups. There is no protection from their mother's milk against diseases any more. This is why the first vaccinations are needed now. In order to be registered the pups have to be tattooed or microchipped. This will be done at your home when the pups have reached the age of seven to nine weeks. When the pups are some eight to ten weeks old they can go to their new owners.

A proud mother with her offspring

IMPORTANT ADDRESSES

American Kennel Club
www.akc.org

Golden Retriever Club of America
www.grca.org

Golden Retriever Foundation
www.goldenretrieverfoundation.org

Orthopedic Foundation for Animals
www.offa.org

Golden Retriever Club of America – National Rescue
Committee
www.grca-nrc.org

ACKNOWLEDGEMENTS AND PICTURE SOURCES

The publisher and author wish to express their thanks to all those who have contributed to the creation of this publication. A special debt of gratitude is due to the following people and organizations: Gé and Ria Kleynen, Toon and Sjannie Roefs-de Kok, and Rolf and Mieke Sorber, on whose premises the majority of the pictures of dogs were taken; Van Riel Distripet in Waalwijk (Netherlands); Dynabone in Kruisland (Netherlands) for providing the products pictured; J.W.H.M. Strikkers for his expert and clear explanations in chapter 13.

All photographs were taken by Esther Verhoef, except for those provided by Ria and Gé Kleynen on pages 29, 31, 113, 118, 120, 122, 123, 124, and the top of page 125.